MADE
FLESH

Craig Arnold

Copper Canyon Press

Port Townsend, Washington

Made Flesh was originally published by Ausable Press in 2008.

Cover art: "Edith in Panama, Complex Foliage," by Emmet Gowin, 2004
Unique gold-toned salt print on handmade paper. 15.5″ × 10.25″

Author photo: Amanda Abel
Design and composition by Ausable Press
The type is Perpetua with Perpetua Titling.
Cover design by Rebecca Soderholm

Copper Canyon Press is in residence at Fort Worden State Park in Port Townsend, Washington, under the auspices of Centrum. Centrum is a gathering place for artists and creative thinkers from around the world, students of all ages and backgrounds, and audiences seeking extraordinary cultural enrichment.

LIBRARY OF CONGRESS CATALOGING-IN-PUBLICATION DATA
Arnold, Craig
Made flesh / Craig Arnold.
p. cm.

ISBN 978-1-931337-42-7 (pbk. : alk. paper)
1. Love poetry.   1. Title.
PS3551.R4835M33 2010
811'.54—dc22   2009043648

COPPER CANYON PRESS
Post Office Box 271
Port Townsend, Washington 98368
www.coppercanyonpress.org

In memoriam
Thom Gunn
(1929-2004)

All of us maidens in a delightful meadow
. . . were playing and picking lovely flowers with our hands,
mingling soft crocuses and irises with hyacinths
and the flowers of the roses and lilies, a wonder to the eye,
and the narcissus which the wide earth grows crocus-colored.
So I myself was picking them with joy, but the earth beneath
gave way and from it the mighty lord and All-receiver
leaped out. He carried me under the earth in his golden chariot,
though I resisted and shouted with shrill voice.
I am telling you the whole truth, even though it grieves me.

——*Hymn to Demeter*

...Cesó todo y dejéme,
dejando mi cuidado
entre las azucenas olvidado.

Everything stopped and I left myself,
leaving my care
forgotten among the lilies.

——San Juan de la Cruz

MADE FLESH

INCUBUS

The chain uncouples, and his jacket hangs
on the peg over hers, and he's inside.

She stalls in the kitchen, putting the kettle on,
buys herself a minute looking for two
matching cups for the lime-flower tea,
not really lime but linden, heart-shaped leaves
and sticky flowers that smell of antifreeze.
She talks a wall around her, twists the string
tighter around the teabag in her spoon.
But every conversation has to break
somewhere, and at the far end of the sofa
he sits, warming his hands around the cup
he hasn't tasted yet, and listens on
with such an exasperating show of patience
it's almost a relief to hear him ask it:
If you're not using your body right now
maybe you'd let me borrow it for a while?

It isn't what you're thinking. No, it's worse.

Why on earth did she find him so attractive
the first time she met him, propping the wall
at an awkward party, clearly trying to drink
himself into some sort of conversation?
Was it the dark uncomfortable reserve
she took upon herself to tease him out of,
asking, Are you a vampire? *That depends,*
he stammered, *are you a virgin?* No, not funny,

1

but why did she laugh at him? What made her think
he needed her, that she could teach him something?
Why did she let him believe that she was drunk
and needed a ride home? Why did she let him
take off her shirt, and fumble around a bit
on the spare futon, passing back and forth
the warm breath of a half-hearted kiss
they kept falling asleep in the middle of?
And when he asked her, why did she not object?
I'd like to try something. I need you to trust me.

Younger and given to daydreams, she imagined
trading bodies with someone, a best friend,
the boy she had a crush on. But the fact
was more fantastic, a fairy-tale adventure
where the wolf wins, and hides in the girl's red hood.
How it happens she doesn't really remember,
drifting off with a vague sense of being
drawn out through a single point of her skin
(a bedsheet threaded through a needle's eye)
and bundled into a body that must be his.
Sometimes she startles, as on the verge of sleep
you feel yourself fall backward over a brink,
and she snaps her eyelids open, to catch herself
slipping out of the bed, her legs swinging
over the edge, and feels the sudden sick
split-screen impression of being for a second
both she and her.
                        What he does with her
while she's asleep, she never really knows,
flickers, only, conducted back in dreams:
Walking in neighborhoods she doesn't know

and wouldn't go to, overpasses, ragweed,
cars dry-docked on cinderblocks, wolf-whistles,
wanting to run away and yet her steps
planted sure and defiant. Performing tasks
too odd to recognize and too mundane
to have made up, like fixing a green salad
with the sunflower seeds and peppers that she hates,
pouring on twice the oil and vinegar
that she would like, and being unable to stop.
Her hands feel but are somehow not her own,
running over the racks of stacked fabric
in a clothing store, stroking the slick silk,
teased cotton and polar fleece, as if her fingers
each were a tongue tasting the knits and weaves.
Harmless enough.
                    It's what she doesn't dream
that scares her, panic she can't account for, faces
familiar but not known, déjà vu
making a mess of her memory, coming to
with a fresh love-bite on her left breast
and the aftershock of granting another's flesh,
of having gripped, slipped in and fluttered tender,
mmm, unbraided, and spent the whole slow day
clutching her thighs to keep the chafe from fading,
and furious at being joyful, less
at the violation, less the danger, than the sense
he'd taken her enjoyment for his own.
That was the time before, the time she swore
would be the last—returning to her senses,
she'd grabbed his throat and hit him around the face
and threw him out, and sat there on the floor
shaking. She hadn't known how hard it was
to throw a punch without pulling it back.

Now, as they sit together on her couch
with the liquid cooling in the stained chipped cups
that would never match, no matter how hard
she stared at them, he seems the same as ever,
a quiet clumsy self-effacing ghost
with the gray-circled eyes that she once wanted
so badly to defy, that seemed to see her
seeing him—and she has to admit, she's missed him.
Why? She scrolls back through their conversations,
searching for any reason not to hate him.
She'd ask him, What's it like being a girl
when you're not a girl? His answers, when he gave them,
weren't helpful, so evasively poetic:
It's like a sponge somebody else is squeezing.
A radio tuned to all stations at once.
Like having skin that's softer but more thick.

Then she remembers the morning she awoke
with the smear of tears still raw across her cheeks
and the spent feeling of having cried herself
down to the bottom of something. Why was I crying?
she asked, and he looked back blankly, with that little
curve of a lip that served him for a smile.
Because I can't.
                    And that would be their secret.
The power to feel another appetite
pass through her, like a shudder, like a cold
lungful of oxygen or hot sweet smoke,
fill her and then be stilled. The freedom to fall
asleep behind the blinds of his dark body
and wake cleanly. And when she swings her legs
over the edge of the bed, to trust her feet

to hit the carpet, and know as not before
how she never quite trusted the floor
to be there, no, not since she was a girl
first learning to swim, hugging her skinny
breastless body close to the pool-gutter,
skirting along the dark and darker blue
of the bottom dropping out—
                              Now she can stand,
and take the cup out of his giving hand,
and feel what they have learned inside each other
fair and enough, and not without a kind
of satisfaction, that she can put her foot
down, clear to the bottom of desire,
and find that it can stop, and go no deeper.

COUPLE FROM HELL

THAT I could tell you this
and not make up stories
That I could break the vow of silence
and speak of the double-bind of couplehood
It seems impossible to say
truly and kindly   but if I could
I would unlock for you
the gates of horn and ivory
that keep you in the underworld
for better and for worse
I would walk you through
another story   older but still true
of two gods bound to each other's need
held hostage to the taste of a pomegranate seed

Peel this fist of a fruit
knuckle by knuckle open
Reveal the blood-drop seeds
like a clutch of frog egg jelly
packed with the tight intensity of tears
that do not want to be released
A hand that opens   as if to ask
Take me out of myself   unclasp
my precious privacies   a hand that waits
cupped and trembling to accept them
slipped like pearls loosened from oyster's flesh
A hand that offers and a hand that takes   the yield
the tender exchange of skin   the terrible surrender

At first you answer Yes   I will belong to this
At first you find yourself naked and self-forsaken
trusting your feet to a lightless floor   but when you awaken
into the prose of after   broken into   broken in
then will you empty your hand of all you were given
afraid   ashamed   to own the joy you held

SHE is Persephone
with a lapful of flowers
with a light foot and an easy faith
that the grass will take her feet without bending
She floats across the surface of a musing
a boat over a quiet pond
sunglare on the water
sun caught in her hair
Last week there was a soup of tadpoles
plump like commas   busy becoming frogs
legs barely budded   they kicked themselves
out of the shadow she cast across them
But today the pond is dry   at the feet of the long stems
there is only a taste of mud to show where the water was

Where are the frogs now
Where is the green water
that waved her gently over them
Where is the boat that drifted with the wind
whichever way   the frogs are gone
and she was just beginning to give them her attention
All over the world frogs are dying
The lilies in her hand are wilting
Once they shook open their pale yellow bells
Now she has plucked the stars that made the sky most lively

Now the leaf-edges are sharp and hurtful
Now there are two crows perched on a burnt fence
facing the other way   pretending not to see
Now she can smell the black god upon her
feel his palms pressed to her temples
making her breath not worth taking
giving her body back to gravity

ALL she wanted was the flowers
yellow and white and wet with dew
but she pulled the dirt like a blanket overhead
and sank down to the underworld with you

The ruby-colored seeds you counted
onto her tongue   they seemed at first so sweet
so bitter when she bit them   Why did she take the bait
Why can't she go back to the way it never was

She has outgrown the pot   root-bound
yellow-leaved   the lightless years have made her
tight with spring   a sprout coiled inside a bean
She aches to explode in red and suicidal bud

Splinter a bone and it will mend
stronger than ever   scrape the skin
and it will scar   even the brain
whose threads unravel can be knit again

But the heart loves the sound of its own breaking
It circles itself in a knot of ice and glass and steel
a kaleidoscope that she never tires of turning over
What can hurt her deeply enough to heal

YOU are Hades
brooding over your lightless kingdom
with a cigarette between your lips like a little fuse
with a stone bowl the color of a bruise
behind your eyes   it fills faster than you can empty
You want someone to come and help you spill it

Through miles of dirt and roots
you felt her fingers tug at the lily-stems
so you cloaked yourself in melancholy glamour
and swam up through the earth to meet her
You never dreamed she would take the arm you offered
spilling a whole field of flowers out of her lap

But your house is never warm   never enough room
She sits all day beside the window   holding her breath
to keep the pane from misting   nothing appears to touch her
any comfort you offer she resists

Each day your hands are more afraid of being fists
Each day you flake off little arrowheads of anger
to flick in her direction   careful each time to miss
the burden you can't bear to keep or lose

SHE naps at all hours
wanting to sleep for weeks
for years   forever   and when she wakes
she is twice as tired   twice as worn away
What should I do   you ask one of the shadows
condemned to live in your lightless country
He stands up to his waist in a pool of clear water
under a tree whose boughs are heavy with yellow peaches
When the water's high he reaches for the fruit
when the branch bends he stoops to drink
Once you taste the nectar that gives gods their life
you live forever   longing for what you can't reach

She keeps you up talking
deep into the night
encircled by the bedside lamp
as if it were the world's only light
and all that she piles on you in her despair
has faded in her memory by morning
What should I do   you ask the ladies-man
who charmed the Mother-goddess into bed
with an old spell   a wryneck bird
pinned by its wings to a little wheel
but when he boasted   the queen of heaven heard
and she nailed him to a wheel of fire   spinning and burning

They know the secrets of unsatisfied desire
the weight that hangs so heavy on her heart
a tear that can't gather the strength to drop
but they are so absorbed in their punishments
pains like nobody else's   all they can spare
are tired expressions of heroic pity

SUNDOWN you come to sit
in the grass beside the stream
to tell each other stories
and watch the purple butterflies
browse for nectar in the meadows
and the green spiders weave webs
between the mullein stalks   waiting
to catch them when they fly too close

Last night she had a dream
of three bright boats in a harbor
wandering lively at the edge of sight
Imagine what the world might open onto
But of what lies beyond the brink
of your shadow-life   past the river
behind the slim limbs of the willows
you can't permit each other even to think

Spring scratches on the door with muddy claws
for you to open   her story is faraway and small
The meadow ticks impatiently   like a hot car cooling
Your attention fails   you tear the grass up by the roots
you break sticks into smaller sticks of the same length
And into your talk the stream insinuates its soft
forgetful laughter   flowing you can't imagine where

Say something please   something to break the silence
something to stop me leaning out and falling in
If you don't hold me back   I don't know what I'll do
Dare you to jump   I dare you   jump or I'll push you in
jump so I can save you   so I can jump in after

COMING home after a party
among the sad shades of the underworld
who drink not to forget but to remember
She drives   turning the wheel with her whole body
Your match keeps missing the cigarette

Her voice comes from a continent away
saying how soft those lips   how many times
they moved her   made her fit so perfectly
into her own skin   the wonder of it lost
word by word in the telling   as she grieves
the loss of a joy that you can never share
your face crumples   paper licked by flame

and when the howl and dazzle of the train
bears down on you   she doesn't even stop
She throttles between the red eyes of the gates
face in the dashboard underwater green
and out of every crevice of the car
moths pour   a cloud of terrible thoughts
wings that patter blindly against your face
brown and numberless as last autumn's leaves

She could put out her hand and save you
loosen a single finger from her fist
but no   she lets you slip beneath the surface
and leaves you drowning in yourself
and all you can comprehend is water
water cut by the scissors of your feet

APRIL   flush with spring
you sprawl across the lawn
under the sycamores   you smoke
and flick the ashes   you try to talk yourselves
out of your cigarettes   out of your lovers
out of your own heads   hoping the heat
of so much conversation might
render the matter   as fat from meat

There is a dead bird in your ear
The air is wrapped around your temples tight
There are so many manners you have tried
without a map to put yourselves aside
To quit this love that is all friction
the push to prove that you are more
solid than the casual clouds
the loose associations of the shore

You talk and talk   your voices always
patient and pleasant   but every word
glitters   a long flake of glass
a knife to sacrifice each other's heart
to the Left-Handed Hummingbird

The pavement scintillates with ants
carrying crumbs of dirt   and your eyes
are fat with not weeping   milkweed
makes froth of the grass   and you are firm
taking a kind of comfort from not yielding

If only some other god could come
and with a touch transform your limbs to tree
and harden your skin to bark   better to be
tormented with the ache of bud and blossom
a green twig   twisted and not breaking

ONCE you have sealed the borders of your bodies
once you cannot release them into a lover's custody
all that is left for love is to be committed
like madmen to the lonely privacy of cells
Drink conversation down to the bottom of the cup
and still there will be silences that words can't drown
still the blood will beat on the doors you don't answer
all of the doors to ecstasy that you have shut

Two people on a bed   trying to make love
your hands won't hold each other   you turn away
to separate sleep   only to startle yourselves awake
in the thick of coupling   arms and mouths
full of each other   some unspeakable desire
grinds you against each other like continental plates
at the world's foundation   but waking once again
you pull apart   to opposite corners of the heart
and what you don't say is a dance floor between you

Soft as ivy pulling brick to pieces
she puts down roots in you   you fear
her hold on you is all that keeps you whole
and fear leads to shame   and shame to anger
and anger to bitterness   she must own
what she has broken   you will hold her
hostage to your unhappiness

TWO in the purple morning
she digs herself so deep
into the burrow of her despair
nothing you say can coax her out of it
Her sadness is as heavy as a planet
and you are a moon caught in orbit
pulled behind her as she paces
restlessly from room to room
Heroically composed you hover
lean in the frame of every door
Your noises of reason and reassurance
only agitate her more
and she will not keep still
will not be talked into an answer
she only pushes you aside
shaking her head No

Then you begin to panic
to threaten and smooth over
snapping at her to pack her bags
to please not walk away from a conversation
She backs into the bathroom   into the bath
you sit beside her wildly talking and talking
What can she do to close her ears
she holds her head under the soapy water
and won't come up for air
and that is when you drag her
out of the tub   that is when you slap her
that is when the blue bruise
ripens   the lid of her lovely eye
a small and perfect plum
and you collapse in fear

How did you two become
dark god and broken blossom
You make her cry to give her comfort
She casts a shadow for you to brood beneath
You prompt each other in a whisper
feeding each other lines until you know
the parts by heart   and with this act
commit a single stroke of self-conviction
nothing can take back

YOU walk out in the morning
and the sky is broad and blue
and across the pathway threads of silk
glint in the sun   at the end of each a spider
still wet from the egg   spins out a dragline
and sails off into the breeze
The air is so bright and busy
your whole body feels it
a puppet weightless on its wires
and you let it guide you down a path
you've never taken   along the river
the little harbor at its mouth
where three blue boats are moored
at a dock cushioned with old tires
where the only sound is the deep bass
drumming of waves on wood

Here is a small café
opening for breakfast
a zinc counter catching the light
at every angle in bright rings of glitter
A cup of black coffee is placed before you
brimming with rainbow-colored foam
a packet of sugar   a pat of butter
a split roll of bread
scored and toasted and still warm
The butter is just soft enough to spread
the coffee hot and sugared to perfect sweetness
the bread grilled to the palest brown
crisp but not quite dry
You tear it neatly into pieces
eat them slowly   when you finish
you are exactly full

Here are bread butter and coffee
Here you are   your own body
eating and drinking what you are given
as one day you in turn will be devoured
and that is all   You were never the lord
of a lightless kingdom   any more
than she has ever been its queen
and the world you talked into a prison
suddenly seems to be made of glass
and your eyes see clear to the horizon
and you feel the molecules of air
part like a curtain   as if to let you pass

DRIVING into the sun
a day clean of meaning
your face raw in the cold light
your eyes dry with the dirt of lost sleep
you feel like you could smile with your whole body
Sunflowers leaning in a field
lift their faces to see you pass
mild   without rebuke
Questions of leaving and arriving
fade to the edges   like a film of mist
across a sun-warm windshield
Will you stop for breakfast
It is sure to be the best
bread and coffee you've ever tasted
Or you could keep driving

Once it delighted you to stare
into the eager face of the girl beside you
to see yourself so perfectly reflected
and so you held each other captive
a pair of mirrors   a tunnel into nothing
Now in the hour you pass in silence
sitting apart together   she seems to glow
with new translucence   moon through clouds
a candle flame in a well of wax
a stained-glass window laced
with sky the color of orchids
leaf the color of lake
lake the color of storm cloud
smoke-colored lilac   irises
the purple of ripe grapes

The story lies open between you
You could pick up where you left off
and soldier on   and make some honor
of being coupled to desperation
Or like two kids who suddenly agree
the game is pointless and no fun
you could quit playing   without regrets
without reprisals   saying simply
Let's get out of here   Yes let's

ASUNDER

A glass is offered   look
Take it before it falls and shatters
Take it firmly or it will slip
out of your fingers   but too strong a grip
will break it   even the warmth of your hand
might swell it so abruptly that
it pulls itself to pieces   Put it down
you've held it too long already
but there is no place safe to put it down
no one to pass it to   no one to share
the burden of such lightness   such
eggshell fragility   It's going to break
sooner or later   better to smash it now
and get it over with   better to be kind

And it was beautiful   and it could hold
all of your heart's blood without spilling
It fit the palm of your hand exactly

But now it lies in pieces   now it points
all of its bright knives at you
Now it is broken   now it is all ruined

MY love is sick   she has begun to turn
inward upon herself   body peeled back
A rubber glove off of a stranger's hand
The seen growing so many sharp edges

My love is sick   she bleeds with strange
irregular terror hard contained
breathes bubbles into her own blood
The bottle mouth is chipped   where is the missing glass

My love is sick and who can help
It is not I that put this sickness into her
I tell myself   it is not I
It does not help either of us   the telling

My love is sick and I would hold her
about the collarbones   hold her down
if she would let me   but between our skins
a storm roars in a film of air

My love is sick and I'm afraid   afraid
her fear is stronger than my fear for her
and so we are made separate by fear
and so we are afraid and not together

FIREFLIES in the drowsy grass
in the trees' hair   signal and answer

I pluck one out of the air
and make my hand a lantern   look

they are so quick   and so many
the field is all a mica-glitter

It is a field where you too
stood once   your dappled body

contours I would dearly call
back to my fingers   I have kept you

cupped in my hand   a captive glow
all of you that still sparkles

For your sake I loved summer
wearing whatever   always sweaty

but not caring   I think we shared
a longing for kindness and cold water

green water   rayed by sunlight
water that lets the body rest

from holding itself up   I think we shared
a bedtime story and a lullaby

I think one day you talked me into buying
a white linen shirt   because it fit

I think that night for the first time
I held you with whole hands   that night

you said   My body will answer yours
that it was like a prayer   why

did I laugh then   when you had let me see
through the idea of you   to you

ON the fire escape of your rented room
we sat and felt the empty city
sweat and fret   we passed a cigarette
back and forth   as once we passed
words like these between us   without
hope of keeping
                        Now I write
without hope of answer   to say
that what we gave each other nakedly
was too much and not enough
To say that since we last touched
I am not empty   I hear you named
and my heart starts   the pieces of your voice
you left   are interleaved with mine

and to this quick spark in the emptiness
to say Yes   I miss how love
may make us otherwise

MUSE   we make our occupation
breaking ourselves against you   bottles
cracked on a ship's prow   christening
new each time   names painted over names
not one of which will stick   and still

we beg to be seduced   and you oblige
you teach us all your tricks   to be alone
and need our solitude   and not to talk
to lose tickets and tokens   to contemplate
the air about us   colorless as tears

to lie   to make love standing up
to write letters and burn them   last of all
to be abandoned   to stand alone
on castle walls that the wind peels apart
to empty gaps between impermeable stone

To stare at the ivy-heavy trees
the galaxies put forth in every leaf
and see no blonde angels' faces
behind their raw transparency
and come always at last to grief

What would we do without you   dance
on sunlit ruins   self-possessed
lie back in our pleasure boats
on our made lakes   trail our fingers
feel the little ripples lapse

and level again to calm behind us
We would be smooth and slick and perfect
and we would never break   if you did not
break us   how would we ever open
if not to you   then who

MISTRAL

SPEEDING across the wide white
slate of the salt flat once   you passed a car
flipped over   you saw the skidmarks
Here the driver took the curve too fast
fishtailed across the shoulder   here he startled
pulled the wheel too hard   spun
suddenly into a blank without horizon
leaving a long scar in the crystal crust

What color car   or who was hurt
are not given for you to know
All you recall are the crates of apples
stacked in the back   that blasted out
of every broken window   spattered
as drops of blood across a snow

IT was a car that did you in
a station wagon   square and German
the size of a small tank   with doors that close
with the satisfying chunk of a bank vault
impervious to small arms fire   and green

This devilish and much to be desired
car   whose sole purpose is to tempt you
into folly   this car is up for sale
by a German   also much to be desired
six feet of blond with a superhero jaw
The girls hold cigarettes for him to light
almost resentfully   you look at him
it makes you want to wade into the gene pool
with your pockets loaded full of rocks

But over the horizon to the east
where the mountain peaks are white with snow
and the slopes are white with almond trees
Granada waits   palaces   poetry
So you hand over a stack of bills as thick
as the phonebook of a small Midwestern city
It is the picture of simplicity

To register you must be resident
explains the man with coffee-colored eyes
at the DMV   he is so helpful
For residence you must obtain
gainful employment   says the woman
at city hall   her cinnamon-bun of hair
is pinned in place with a pair of lacquer chopsticks
Tourist   she says with sad sweet malice
is not gainful employment   and did you know

your visa's valid only two more weeks
Granada is further away than you imagined
but you can do this   you are on a roll
Another German   this town is overrun
will let you teach in his little English school
but the students make you nervous   faces
turning to follow you like sunflowers
and why are they all named María

The Germans are smiling at you a lot
more than they used to   you suspect them
of bureaucratic sympathies   There is
a man in Puerto   they say   he fixes things
problems like these   he is very sympathetic
You drive to Puerto thinking of Granada
Granada   and not the Guardia Civíl
waiting to pull you over   they will see
expired plates and visa   march you
into the sunflowers and nonchalantly
shoot you   like poor García Lorca
It is a miracle but you elude them

The man who fixes things is fat
with a cowboy hat and a belt buckle
the shape and size of Texas   he leans back
as if to admire the mess you've made
from the best angle   Sell the car
to a friend   he says   then borrow it
You have exactly such a friend
happy to buy   at half the price you paid
a mucus-green Mercedes   with room aplenty
for wife and four or is it five kids
you can't keep count   they're always moving

Old man he says   I can't   I'm sorry
You could run over some old lady
and I'd be liable   I can't afford it
and though you swear eternal mindfulness
of all old ladies   Granada is receding
into the distance   down the wrong
end of the telescope you are beginning
to feel your head is in   but yes
yes   of course   you understand

And after all this you need a break
so you decide to roast a batch of peppers
and you are standing at the sink
slipping them out of their burned skins
with bone-cold water running over your hands
when like Narcissus staring in the pond
you feel yourself contracting to a small
circle of face that you can't see beyond

Something is going wrong   you can't stop
paying attention   you have fallen
into an ever-present consciousness

a feeling that doesn't go away
next morning   or the next one   or the next

THERE is a circle drawn around you
no one will enter   as if you'd caught
the moon   and swung it about your body
Everyone smiles and smiles at you
as if you knew something that they don't
and they know it   and you don't

It's the *mistral*   María says
the dirty wind that blows from Africa
This is as good an explanation
as any   you are beginning to love
explanations   they make you feel
expansive   they make things fit together

But your hat   you lost it in the crowd
it disappeared   there were so many feet
and now it's gone   the cap you swore
however black and tattered   you would keep
One thing at least you'd be responsible for
Now it is lost and it taught you nothing

You go out to search the streets
but there is Jesus   carried along
on a big bed   there is his mother
another María   there are legs
behind those little curtains   they shuffle
forward and sway   the baby-elephant walk

Everything stops   everyone sort of
hangs around   waiting for something
to happen   a man in a pointed hood
fishes in his pocket for a match
The wind has blown his candle out
He asks his neighbor for a light

The only movements with any purpose
are those the children make   breaking
out of the crowd   to scrape the cobbles
clean of the spills of still-warm wax
and roll it into balls   they show them off
argue which one has got the biggest

You are deep in this fit of noticing
when without ado or explanation
somebody hands your hat to you
and walks off   there are flecks of mud
sprinkled across the brim   that someone
meaning well   has tried to brush away

Oh you are so immensely grateful
Your heart swells   and you stand there
thanking and thanking   somebody knew
whose hat it was   is looking out for you
not from love or concern   but because
that is what happens   what we do

You maybe could get used to this
not worrying   you could let it go
these thirty years of making fists
glue-thick in a bowl of dough
each time you try to scrape it off
one hand   it sticks to the other

but when you work it long enough
what happens   it begins to bind
pulls away from your fingers   takes
itself to itself   and is its own thing
separate   and marvelous smooth
and you no longer notice yourself breathing

EASTER Monday   the sun lies
evenly on the pale stones
on the walls   white as the last snow
left in the shadowed hollow of a hill
on the cobbles   a thin shine of wax
that makes tires squeak as they turn corners

Look   there are pink geraniums
hooked in pots to the plaster   one
has dropped and shattered on the pavement
It might have hit anyone   but didn't
This town is full of falling pots and tiles
not hitting anyone   how wonderful

Look   here is a shop that sells
soup bowls   colored the clear yellow
of aspen leaves loosening on the stem
and stained with blushes of deep green
They fit your palms so perfectly
Why don't you buy them   help your hands
remember the curves of asking and accepting

Look in this little church   the shadows
give away slowly the flash and glitter
of gold paint   picked out by candles
Look   a rack of electric votives
coin-operated prayers   how splendid
Coin after coin you feed it   try
to guess which bulb will light up next

Look   little miracles of silver
they pin up for the blesséd virgin

that she deliver them of their afflictions
eyes   ears   hands   breasts with tiny nipples
Look at the saint in the glass case
incorrupt   you can see his long arm-bones
under a skin of silk   so cobweb-frail
the warm cloud of a breath might melt it

Look there   among the candle stubs
facing the corner   there is María
waiting for someone to put her back
in her proper alcove   A plastic tear
trickles   like sap from a cut pine
down her cheek   the color of a tusk

Over her flat chest   the folds
of periwinkle silk are pinned in place
with a hairclip from the five & dime
the kind that schoolgirls like to wear
spelling their names in rhinestone   hers
says she is not María   but Soledad

It makes you silly   everything you see
swirling with rainbows   like a film
of oil on water   the way she stands
the wings of a wind-bedraggled bird
it makes you want to take her hands
and lead her for a twirl across the floor

She's lit with the same gleam of pebbles
upon the beach   in the tide-pools
you used to comb for opalescent beach-glass
a child   barely able to make a sentence
to say how cold the water was

Each time you came upon a piece
that the sand had not yet ground and polished
you put it back in the ocean   thinking
you'd find it later   when it was finished

YOUR friend's arriving on the bus
at six AM   and you will go to meet her
because you are your own puppet
can stop bullets   and you would never
get lost   the street map of the world
is wired into your brain   and anyway
it is all a big adventure   and the wrong
bus station   but you don't know that yet

Here is the statue of Queen What's-her-name
green with a copper-polished nose
Here is the market but no vegetables
The boarded-up stalls are looking
uncomfortable   here is the cathedral
here is the square   smack in the middle
here is the couple fucking   half-undressed
skin on the flagstone   Aren't they cold
Couldn't they find even a patch of grass

Here is the bus station but where are the buses
Why are the windows all so starry-eyed
A bus would be too sad to come here

Here is a man falling in step
beside you   his hair is full of eagles
Spare change he says   You give him some
No not enough   he says   but you don't have
anything more to give him   No I want
your wallet   Yes your wallet   I've got a
something   What the something is
you don't appreciate   remember this
is all in Spanish   probably something sharp

Why don't you run   Don't run   he calls
across three lanes of traffic and the strip
of grass between them and the three
lanes of traffic going the other way
Lucky for you there aren't so many cars

Two garbagemen in orange uniforms
are working down the street   They look
conspicuous   better to walk beside them
looking   you hope   conspicuous   at least
by association   They don't seem to mind

Perhaps you are too tall for walking
Here you hail a cab and tell the driver
The bus station please   and not that one
the other bus station   do you know where
and he says No   why don't we check
the phone book   You've been here six months
and never seen a phone book   but no doubt
he has a better idea of where to find one
being a cab driver   and one would hope
knowledgeable about such things
Besides you need to find a cash machine
You don't have any money left to pay him

Here is a bar   phonebook cash and coffee
all together   what a stroke of luck
You're ready to rumble   but now the driver
gets in an argument about the Basques
bombing another car   you so hate
to interrupt   and it is only after
three cups of coffee that all parties

are satisfied
You'd like to meet the Basques
They look like they are into heavy metal
and have ideas about destruction
Maybe your mugger was a Basque
and that was why you didn't understand
the something
Here is the station and her bus
has just pulled up to the platform
hours late   What timing   if you had gone
straight to the right place you would have only
waited for hours   and never been
so wonderfully abstracted by the Basques
the fare   the phonebook   and the orange men
and the running away in sheer adrenal terror
from the mugger with that something you will spend
hours over the dictionary
hoping to decode
and yes those two
not minding where they made a kind of love

Of course you could have eaten breakfast
smoked a pack of the nasty cigarettes
and made new words for songs
The pain in Spain falls mainly on the sane
or some such variation   and no doubt
time would have run on swimmingly

Isn't it sweet when everything works out

IN the Patio of Orange Trees
where the white petals drop and drift
in the fountains   you can leave your shoes
and wander barefoot through the galleries
where the floor is cool and smooth and welcoming
where the brickwork arches on the mismatched pillars
each have a band of dark slick stone
at waist-height   polished by centuries
of palms passing
                    Outside the mosque
a bus is waiting   it's the last
bus of the day   and you were lucky
to find a seat   you're off to the ruined city
you don't know how you will return

Across the aisle a young Australian
reads aloud from his big guidebook
the story of the caliph's foreign bride
The country where she came from   in the mountains
the snow never melted   she got so homesick
her husband   a romantic kind of bloke
planted her groves of almond trees
When the spring came   all the slopes
were white with blossom   his girlfriend nestles closer
under his arm
                  There are no almonds now
only a heap of honey-colored rocks
the bones of buildings   a single arch
like the keyhole for a giant door
a courtyard paved with white marble
a long pool running down the middle
hedged with the warm green of myrtle
a fish rises through the murky water
to nose the surface   making a single ripple

Here on the last puzzle-piece of wall
the plaster's molded in designs
of knots and tangles   like the graffiti tags
scribbled in quick unbroken strokes
across bridges and subway cars
They are   your heart stutters to see
the letters of another alphabet
a vast lace of calligraphy
a hundred thousand characters of praise

When you look up   the wind has changed
as sudden as the twisting of a lens
back into focus   everywhere you look
seems otherwise   you no longer
see yourself over your own shoulder
in the second person   you have snapped
back into your body
                        Oh my god
where have I been   To pay the world
so much attention   Where have I been
To be your own puppet   Where
have I been   To fall and let yourself
be caught   Where have I been   To god and back

A PLACE OF FIRST PERMISSION

(A memorable fancy for my Lady Jane)

First to blossom   the pear trees
     are white   the shape of candle flames
Their boughs are bent and darkened by the rain

It's April   you're riding on a train
     with a green of leaf-opening
         and a slow cadence of wire outside your window
     Your tongue is bowing a note across a broken
         corner of tooth
             and as you move
the track's percussion catches up to the beat of a song
     that's looped in your memory all morning long
         even the beads of water weaving
     over the glass
             drop into its groove

You came downtown for a lunch date
     with an old teacher   and you were late
and the meal was punctuated by impatient
     looks at the clock   and your attempts at talk
         grew more and more awkward   and each missed beat
     in the conversation made it worse
         and you left in sadness and defeat
You are headed back to dinner now
     with your first love   the one you never
         quite got over   whose face
     leans in over the shoulder

of every love you've held in place of her
　　whispering *Why* and *What if*
whose memory turns up like a bright coin
　　in the pocket of a coat you haven't
　　　　worn for years　　a comfort and a curse

In a car full of unfriendly eyes
　　passing a pale gray town somewhere between
　　　　failure and desolation　　you sit in a corner
　　trying to make yourself smaller
mouthing the words of a song
　　to give your breath something to hold
Cheek to the window　　you can smell the cold
　　on the far side of the glass
　　　　　　　　　　Across from you
a man yokes one arm
　　around the neck of the woman he clearly
　　　　wants the world to know he's married to
She sits tightly　　tries to hide
　　her hesitation at his touch
Her head hangs　　as if her makeup weighs too much
　　a loose lock of her hair keeps
　　　　wandering over her eyes　　but she won't fix it
　　setting your teeth each time she flicks it
　　　　absent-mindedly aside
The way they sit there　　it destroys your heart

Two drops of water wavering back and forth
　　along the glass　　join at last
and run together in a sudden trickle
　　slantwise across the pane
　　　　　　　　And then the train

slows to a stop   sighs out one long breath
and the rain lets its fingers lift
    from the keys of concrete and new leaves
            the oilspots and the gum bullets
        ground into the platform
                            and a girl
gets on the train   confection-pink
    in a poof of sweater   scattering pearls
            out of her clothing and her hair

She pitches into a seat across the aisle
    gives you the corner of a smile
and sets herself to drumming   foot kicking
    a backbeat   her fingers clicking
            the castanet of her heart-locket
    (making the happy-couple photographs inside
            mash lips   over and over)
until at last the cellphone in her pocket
    plinks out the ending of Beethoven's Ninth

        Hearts unfold like flowers before thee

Her cellphone and your memory
    chiming the same tune at the same time
            an accidental rhyme
        of place and grace
                            One moment you are there
hugging the irritation and despair
    close to your skin   a sweater of rough wool
Her voice reaches   takes a loose
    end of the yarn   and gives it a pull
            and the whole mood unknits itself around you

You press the prickle of your skin against
    the air in affection   raw   peeled
        You are a field unfenced
    over which are conducted by the breeze
the smell of the rain-pattered pavement
    slips of whisper wirebrushed on the cymbal of your ear
The bodies of other people near
    you feel without hostility   without resistance
        all equally likely   with their own
    plans and appointments   stops not to miss

As when you put yourself within a kiss
    so perfectly   you lose all definition
        beyond mouth and fingers   moving
    patient and presently and open

        and you are full out to the skin

AS you may dream inside a dream
    you may wake out of waking
the ghostly outline of the scene
    reflected in the glass that the bright lamps
        have made a mirror   is not the 3:15
but a club car   paneled in old oak
    dark with the folds of smoke unscrolled
from cigarettes   with thick wine-colored drapes
    gathered up around the windows
        in velvet ropes   a single lamp
    making a small pool of light on every table

Some kind of party is going on
The car is filled with people   dressed
    to the nines   sipping splendid cocktails
Dancers fizz   like the bubbles struck up
    in a tulip-flute of champagne
They turn in an endless loop   a kaleidoscope
    made of momentary points
        of naked skin
                        bare wrists
slipping out of cuffs   deltas of breastbone
    arms falling against each other   fingertips
testing the soft seam of an elbow
    a hand fanning across the small of back

After a year of swallowing his love
    for his best friend   he's told her all at last
Don't be silly   she answers   and he smiles
    toys with the tassel of a drape
        over the table   making it all he sees
The way his mouth seems to freeze

how soft the cord twisted around his finger
   burgundy was it or maroon
will stay with him all his life

Four girlfriends at the next table
  they want to dance but one of them is shy
The other three have ordered her a drink
  she doesn't like and left her there
    to watch their purses while they hit the floor
Her Cosmopolitan is pink and bitter
  and she begins to hate them buzzing by
    chirping at her to loosen up

One of them conspires to spill her glass
  on a man's sleeve a good excuse
    for a conversation and when he offers
  to buy another how can she refuse
Five Long Islands later locked in the bathroom
  to have a conversation with the mirror
    it frightens her to hear her voice
  like someone else's humming through her bones
Half an hour she stands there watching
  the drift of slur and struggle across her face
    before she remembers where she is
  and fumbles for the latch

The man at the bar looks lost his wife has vanished
  Where has she gone he'd never guess
    she's bumped into an old flame
and after a time of talk and remembered sweetness
  they've slipped away to an empty cabin
    to make the love they left unfinished

Eyes brilliant with excitement
    breath shallow in wonder and disbelief
Oh they are growing dizzy   oh the tips
    of their fingers tingle   oh they go
            under the surface of something   brim
        purple and hurt with happiness
Her white socks are gray at the heel and toe

And maybe when the drunk girl stumbles
    out of the bathroom   breaks in on the lovers
and stares uncomprehendingly a long
    moment   before she turns embarrassed
And after they have quickly dressed
    without enough time even to kiss
maybe he will spend the evening
    yearning to catch her eye and hold it fast

And maybe she will act guilty
    fingering all her zips and buttons
            over and over   worried what will show
    and wanting to mask her afterglow
she guides her shaky legs toward the dance
    and knocks against the table   where
            (you saw this coming)   the quiet girl
    is giving her pink drink a second chance

And maybe the glass will spill and shatter
    and maybe the man rejected
will kneel to help collect the small disaster
    into a napkin   maybe meaning
            nothing more than a kindness   and still their eyes
    thread together   and they are lost

They say the party hasn't started
    till someone breaks a glass   I swear
        I'll kill her   He can always tell
Well did you evah what a swell
    party this is   That dress what was she thinking
Are you hurt   Can you believe they just
Jesus her skin it's like she blushed
    all over when she came   But it
        was worth it   There you are I wondered
    where you were hiding   it's been hours
But it was worth it   wasn't it
    worth it   So sorry   What were you drinking

They may never guess what grooves
    they drop into   whom they bring
        together   or come between   or pass
    unknowingly   wallflowers
        who fall in step   by not stepping
So many voices and courses overlapping
    so many six-petaled flowers
        of silk and crystal   the pieces make
    so many possibilities
        in a handful of broken glass

AT a still point of the turning floor
    there is a dancer   you would know her
        even across a crowded room
    the way she sways is so familiar
She weaves with the easiness and grace
    of someone so completely in
        possession of her body   the beat
        she lays down with her hands and feet
    is all that keeps the cosmos in its groove

She is a lash of flame
    spiraled to fire-colored hair
Her hands unfold a flower out of the air
If you reached out to take it   if you came
    closer   you would liquefy like wax
        pooled in a candle's crater   you would spill
    past possibility of shame
                        She says
Smoke me a bass line to go with that
    thick as blackstrap molasses   she says
Give me the buzz of oboe between your lips
    the tingling tambourines   the sweet
        percussive patter of palm on palm   she says
The whole world is poured into the deep bowl of my hips

Now get on up   she says   and shake
    the creases out of your clothes   she says
        Your life is nothing but the thread
    you spin behind you   every step
        a turn   a loop   a figure-eight
    until the day that blind witch Fate
        opens her scissors and snips you dead

What would you do   if you could take it
     between your fingers   if you could feel
          every knot and snag and tangle
     loosen and gather softly round the spool
What would you do with such permission
     how far would you wind it   what decision
          you made   or didn't make

You can sit the next one out together
     here at this table   you can share
a glass of white vermouth   pretend it's absinthe
     green as venom   green as Eden
     seawater   wormwood   pine-needle
and watch the dramas and the comedies
     playing around you   you can ease
          into one of those silences
     that never feel the need to fill
And you can say what you've been so afraid
     to put in words   what's tied your tongue
          for years of useless reasons and excuses
     the apology you never made

Love   from you I learned
     to dance   you taught me with your body
          and not words   your movement answered
     mine   and mine yours   you gave me back
to my own body   we passed between us
     all the speechless gestures of admiration
          of those early in love   who aren't yet
     careful to say so much and no further

But each time we kissed you kept your lips
     closed   however much I pleaded

Open the petals of your mouth for me
    you never let them part   I thought your heart
        too was closed   I was afraid to see
    how happily you would have offered
        everything   had I done the same

Love forgive me   all I've given
    has been a form of taking
talking over a table of scarred wood
    talking always about the table
I've held out my hand and drawn it back
    in case you took it   always afraid
        to take away the table altogether

You laid a coal on my lips   you made me
    bend my chromatic into blue
You taught me how to spin my line
    back and forth in a broken prayer
        and give it to the all-assuming air
Now here it is   my gift to you
    if you will take it   oh my Ariadne
        my muse   my lady jane   my valentine

She takes your hand   her thumb circles
    lightly over the backs of your fingers
        How have you never noticed
    the sweetest galaxy of freckles
        scattered across the fine skin of her wrist

Outside   the ragged trickle of the rain
    the dark snarl of branches   the blades of grass
        bend and flutter   caught in the wind
    that sweeps over the wake you leave behind

As if it all were bowing briefly
    toward your passage   nodding   as if to say
        Yes   you're going to get away
    with everything
                As if the dancers
happy or disappointed   loving or leaving
    their voices   the red velvet curtain
swaying from side to side   the broken glass
    the girl you loved   and you   and the whole train
        were nothing but a line of thread
    licked   twisted   drawn through
        the eye of a needle   and slowly pulled
another stitch in the cloth of the world
    that is all stitches   a piece of string
        lost in the weave   never to be untangled

Look   did you see it
                The eye blinks
and the bud of the moment blows open
    shakes off its sleepy petals
        and you are sitting there
listening to a girl in a pink sweater
    gossip into a phone
                and she gets off
    at the next stop   (there is no keeping her)
leaving a dimpled seat   a hole
    shaped like her in the air   a long blonde hair

    and the smell of rain in wet wool

HYMN TO PERSEPHONE

Help me remember this   how once the dead were locked
out of the ground   and wandered sleepless and sun-blinded
She was the one who took them each by the hand   helped them
lay their bodies back in the dark sweet decay
gladly   as onto a lover's bed   they call her Koré
the Maiden   a dark queen with a crown of blood-colored poppies
her fingers lift the cool coins from a dead girl's eyelids
her breath in a man's mouth releases him from memory

There was a man who would play fast and loose with Love
She smiled at first to hear him tossing around her nicknames
like cheap wedding confetti   Pretty Butt   Manslayer   Smile-lover
or mocking the blessed valentine folded up in her lap
petal-pink as a seashell   but when he swore he'd never
let Love knock the wind out of him   and leave him panting
that set her teeth on edge   Love is a cruel justice
she makes us pay for our lover's sins as well as our own
and she took away the one whose loss would hurt him deepest

Maybe he would have wept   but grim determination
came to him more easily than tears   and so he followed
the road that only the desperate walk with their eyes open
where the willows bend to comb their fingers through the river
and the long grass cuts the ankles   stalks of mullein
stand like tall candles   the dead mixed with the living
and spiders weave webs between them   glint in the sunlight
the vague gray country where all shadows gather
and the dark queen keeps them safe in her lightless mansion

She was sitting out on her porch   peeling a pomegranate
leaning back in her chair   feet propped on the railing
her face a cool and cloudless moon   ink-black hair
Who are you she called   most of my visitors come here
with their arms crossed and pennies laid over their eyes
My eyes are open he answered   nothing I do can close them
night after night I lie awake   counting my heartbeats
my hands won't work   they can't seem to hold anything

Come in the house then   she held the door half-open
and deep in the dark hallway he thought he could see the faintest
flutter of movement   and he was afraid   She took his hand
her fingers cool as a cave of water-hollowed limestone
Someone you knew she asked   this graceful tender of shadows
My advice to you is to go home and grieve her
Sound the well of your tears as deeply as you can
wipe your eyes   and be glad you're still among the living

Why he demanded   you could bring her back in a heartbeat
Maybe she said   do you think you're the first to come here
chasing after someone they lost   but you have the guilty
look of a man who tossed away what he loved too lightly
How can I feel sorry for you   You don't know the first
thing about my love he snapped   So prove it she said
sing me a love song   who is this girl you miss so much
that you come to my house to fetch her out of the shadows

He sang of the first permission of flesh and flesh to entangle
how we abandon the guard of our heart   and throw our borders
open   and welcome a sweet invader to take possession
the sudden exquisite catch in a throat   and the slow hush
of a breath unfettered   the sweetest sounds to a lover's ear
He sang of hands finding   shyly at first   their way
to another shelf of hips   oh how the heart flares
and melts like wax spilling over a candle's lip

56

Even the spiders stopped spinning their webs to listen
I like your song she said   maybe you'll come back
and sing it again for me before too long   he shivered
Out of her lawn she plucked a withered stem of mullein
Take this and go home   and you'll find her waiting
I'll give you one more day and night and the morning after
to spend together however you please   I warn you though
when the time comes   say your goodbyes   and don't look back

That day the cherry-trees in the square had just flowered
making a roof of white blossom over their heads
That day they walked   with the awkwardness of the long parted
and sat on either side of a table   and shared a pizza
and washed it down with a half-carafe of cheap red wine
and tried to talk their way back into their bodies
and as they left   the leaf-buds were a green promise

and when she stopped to put on more lipstick
she'd left it all printed around the rim of her glass
he laughed and said   There goes my chance to kiss you
Why   she replied   would you ever let that stop you
And they took each other's lips frankly   took their faces
between each other's hands   and the tears were shaken out
like raindrops beaded on a branch   and they were barely
able to have enough of touching   and they kissed each other dry
and over breakfast they smiled   so hard that it hurt

They went to make the bed   and found the sheets bloody
and so they fished through all their pockets for quarters   and walked
down to the corner laundromat   where they sat together
holding hands as they waited and watched the dryer tumble
Together they folded linen   billowed it out between them
to shake away the wrinkles   brought the corners together
in halves   in quarters   their bodies coming at each fold closer
and smiling at each other over the hot cotton

The clock-hand spun in circles   and soon morning was over
and all they had left was the long drive to the airport
the slow walk through the terminal   trying to talk each other
out of sorrow   their voices bright with desperation
until they stood at the edge of what any words could comfort

Don't try to follow me this time she said   whatever
else happens   we made each other happy for a day
Yes he agreed   and they turned to walk away from each other
and though he struggled bravely to keep his face together
he cracked   he ran tear-broken back through the concourse
and caught her up in his arms   until she eased gently
out of his clasp   and kissed him one last time   and left him

But too late   the moment he turned   a demon of memory
sat hard on his shoulder and caught hold of his ear
murmuring over and over the words of their final parting
What   what would've given the story a happier ending

Out in the meadow that day   dark purple butterflies
sipped the sweet nectar from yellow cups of blossom
and blundered into the webs where the big spiders waited
to tuck them into the soft silk of their winding sheets
all their legs a wiggle of happy anticipation
What are you doing here she asked him   not unkindly
You look awful   your eyes are spilling over with memory

The world hurts to look at he said   all glitter and sharp edges
I'm sorry she said   but didn't I warn you to take your time
together   and let it go at that   it would've been kinder
Instead you sent your love back to my mansion   loaded
with twice the grief she left with   her own and yours also
And with that   he felt like he'd fallen into a dark lake
and the cold had got his bones   and he was slipping under
Let me join her then he said   I'm sick of living

No she told him   twice you've come here uninvited
and before I let you lay yourself in my bed forever
go back to the sunlit world   and tell your story
All I can offer you   if you aren't afraid to accept it
is a kind of consolation   and then she gave him a look
that was almost shy   First would you do me a small favor
Make me another song like the last one you sang me
only this time sing to me of self-effacing
surrender of love   that we give knowing we have to lose it

And so he sang of the love that is not so fearful of ending
that fear ends it   love that admits the flavor of pain
the pulling apart of ivy-tendrils ripped from a tree
love that lays itself in the grave of another body
sweetened by loss   as we lose ourselves in our lover's arms
given completely over to pleasure   the dark flower
that opens   petal by petal   unfolding us to the utmost
pitch of surrender   lost in the joy of self-forgetting

Then he praised the maiden who makes us a gift of grieving
to spill the bowl of our tears when it grows too heavy
the grace to release our beloved kindly into her care
and not to fear the soft tap of her footsteps approaching
her fingers touching our eyelids   when she comes to invite us
into her bed   and with cool unhurried hands unravels
the milky threads of our thoughts and memories   may we part with them
gladly   and go more easily into the dark flower

And the girl smiled   as if they'd shared a secret
and she broke the mullein-stalk in half and then in quarters
pressed the pieces into his palm and closed his fingers
Throw these to the wind she commanded   and he did
and they were lost in the long grass that cuts the ankles
Then she reached on her tiptoes   he was a head taller
and breathed into his mouth   the scent of mint and violets

And he woke up alone in the other world   and he was
walking down a familiar street   and it had been raining
all night   and the boughs of the trees were black and heavy
and the first cars of the morning passed   with their tires hissing
over the blacktop   and under his feet he felt the pavement
slither   a carpet of petals battered down by the raindrops
and each puddle swirled with a slick of green-gold pollen
and though he couldn't remember how or when it happened
his heart had been spilled   and at its quick was planted a wet
seed that he'd never known before   and it was spring

MADE FLESH

THAT day drew a broken tower
out of the tarot pack   a plume of flame
and over the wreck a vast flower
with ragged petals of soft white ash
that was once flesh and useless paper
blooming over the postcard-perfect blue

Of all the tiny figures falling
end over end   there were two
who had stepped up holding hands
to give themselves together to the air
A love that   sudden and certainly   I knew
I didn't share and didn't want to share
with anyone but you
                              your sunlit demons
your cigarettes and fire escapes
your petals and grenades   your laugh
like the chime of wind in icicles
the chuckle of fire in ecstasy
of its own burning
                              and at my fingertips
were ten digits you had asked me
never to dial again

And then it seemed my whole head
the dot on this little *i*   would blow
like the puff of a dandelion
And then the seedpods of my eyes
split into tears   and I felt a swift
clutch at my throat   that was the root
of cruelty and tenderness
worming its way in

YOU are the hummingbird that comes
a pure vibration   wings a blur
propeller-burring a million beats
to keep still   the world's littlest pivot
spinning the heaven's hemisphere
as a wineglass with a wet finger
laid on the rim to make it ring

Feathers a rainbow   how you reel
hovering over blossom   cheeks
tucked into the honeysuckle
to lap a single drop of nectar
onto your tongue   messenger-goddess
kicking a gold-dust of pollen
out of your winged heel

The slow promise of your approach
makes my throat thick   the joy gathers
deep in my spine   as if it were a snake
making a smooth wave of muscle
toward the taste of water

HOW have I thought of you
a fire-balloon   a paper lantern
light   hot   thin   lit from within
and liable to burst at any moment
into flame   fine-threaded
textile   spider-silk
I'd put a finger through   without
meaning   all of it lies   and safer
not to touch   not even gingerly
a noli-me-tangere   a shy fern
folding away from a dumb fumble

How new you are   a weave
of nerves and joys   an unexpected
flush of chest   whose nipples two
exquisite freckles more   to make
neat little question marks over   slowly
pink granite   Verona   rock-rose
whose petals bitten   wet the tongue
of a thirst-enslaved traveler
                              Come
I've missed you   bring your breath
ginger-singed   your white lap
come loosen your honey hair
in strands of sap   come trap me in
your amber   in your dappled arms
slide up   sheathe my hips
in yours   please   come

TO be body and nothing else
to sway in bone and muscle   mobile
meaning only ourselves   to need
neither to fumble nor hold on

but simply   lightly   to belong
where we are put   to feel thought
as a fever   a fume   a delirium
a prattle of nerve on nerve   that breaks

like a warm breath over snowflakes
To know existence is just to come
and go   to be a single moment
captured in crystal   and released

the hold of a heart's fist   a jellyfish
fills and deliquesces   a star
flares up fierce and yellow   falls
into itself   collapses   oh

god   the body is all a flower
we bud   we put out petals   swell
with the seed's pulse   loosen our pods
wistfully   wilt on the stem   and drop

once open only to close
our eyes   our stories   to know that this
passing is all   and here to find
if not joy   then a kind of peace

FALL creeps like a slow flame
over a maple   limb by limb
leaves that once fanned their hands
open   wanting to put themselves
all over everything   begin to glow
brave vermilion and lively yellow
let at last their fingers curl
into the palm   and let go

The same fire is touching us
around the edges   licking wrinkles
into the corners of our eyes
making the skin inside our elbows
silky as old coins
                    And when we lie
together   and I feel your bones
blaze   and the rose of your face unfolds
and the incandescence of your skin
crackles   like the paper at the tip
of a drawn-on cigarette   and dies
in a final fluttering of ash

Then   then we feel death
as the deepest coming   then we ease unhurried
into the bud of body   then we learn
little by little   to relinquish
gracefully   and less afraid
each time   to let each other slip
slowly out of our clasp   made
fire   made flower   made flesh

February 14, 2007

ACKNOWLEDGEMENTS

Grateful acknowledgement is made to the editors of the following publications, in which these poems first appeared—in whole or in part, under different titles, arranged in different keys and tempos: *American Literary Review, Barrow Street, Bat City, Borderlands, Colorado Review, Conduit, Denver Quarterly, Euphony, Gulf Coast, Open City, Poetry, Poetry Northwest, Quarterly West, Smartish Pace* and *Yale Review.*

Early mixes of "Muse" ("Asunder") and "To be body and nothing else" ("Made Flesh") first appeared in *Bright Pages: Yale Writers 1701-2001*, edited by J. D. McClatchy (Yale, 2001).

"My love is sick" ("Asunder") first appeared in *The New American Poets,* edited by Michael Collier (Middlebury, 2000).

"Your friend's arriving on the bus" ("Mistral") appeared in *Best American Poetry 2004,* edited by Lyn Hejinian (Scribners, 2004).

"You walk out in the morning" ("Couple from Hell") appeared in *Best American Poetry 2006*, edited by Billy Collins (Scribners, 2006).

The title of "A Place of First Permission" is taken from the poem "Often I Am Permitted to Return to a Meadow" by Robert Duncan. The poem samples briefly from "Joyful, Joyful, We Adore Thee" (words by Henry J. van Dyke), and from Cole Porter's "Did You Evah?" (the Debbie Harry/Iggy Pop version, rather than Crosby/Sinatra).

"Hymn to Demeter" is quoted from Athanassakis, Apostolos N., trans. *The Homeric Hymns,* pp. 13. © 1976 Johns Hopkins University Press. Reprinted with the permission of The Johns Hopkins University Press.

Thanks to Henry Staten, whose *Eros in Mourning* (Johns Hopkins, 1997) first suggested a possible ethos for these poems; to the National Endowment for the Arts, the Texas Institute of Letters, the Princeton University Humanities Council, the MacDowell Colony and the American Academy in Rome, for support that made this book possible, in particular to Carol Rigolot, Paul Muldoon, James Richardson and Dana Prescott, for your hospitality; to Francine Prose, for advice and support when it was most needed; to Mark Strand, for your friendship and the grace of your example; to Jennifer Tonge, for aiding and abetting; to Tim Johnson, for making me see what wasn't finished; and to Rebecca Lindenberg, for making me see what was.

The Chinese character for poetry is made up of two parts: "word" and "temple." It also serves as pressmark for Copper Canyon Press.

Since 1972, Copper Canyon Press has fostered the work of emerging, established, and world-renowned poets for an expanding audience. The Press thrives with the generous patronage of readers, writers, booksellers, librarians, teachers, students, and funders—everyone who shares the belief that poetry is vital to language and living.

Major funding has been provided by:

Amazon.com

Anonymous

Beroz Ferrell & The Point, LLC

Cynthia Hartwig and Tom Booster

Golden Lasso, LLC

Lannan Foundation

National Endowment for the Arts

Cynthia Lovelace Sears and Frank Buxton

Washington State Arts Commission

For information and catalogs:

COPPER CANYON PRESS
Post Office Box 271
Port Townsend, Washington 98368
360-385-4925
www.coppercanyonpress.org